They Don't Know It All...
History Class Live

(Realtime Class Responses)

Tracey M. Downey

They Don't Know It All...
History Class Live
(Realtime Class Responses)

Copyright © 2024 by Tracey M. Downey

Published by: ACH Publishing
www.Achpublishing.com

DEDICATION

To you, my dear students, for making my daily journey worthwhile and for making this book come to life, you will never know how much the laughter and the great discussions fill my soul with happiness. Thank you for being the inspiration for this book, I am forever grateful for being part of your world.

To my two biggest cheerleaders in life, for whom this book would never have come to fruition, had they not constantly pushed me to believe I could. Alexandra, you are my daily reason to wake up and you inspire me to be the best possible version of myself, just so "I'll be" a better example for you! Paul, thank you for always being willing to stand by my side and support me on whatever crazy idea I come up with, you are my rock, and the love of my life! My infinite gratitude and love to you both!

I cannot forget to send a big THANK YOU to Angelique Huerta for doing my Title in her amazing note taking way! I have never had a student who could make grading so much fun, just because of colors and word art! You have made me obsessed with always having colored pens, highlighters, fine point & chunky style markers on hand for every meeting or seminar. Thank you from the bottom of my heart, for helping bring my imagination to life!

A NOTE FROM THE AUTHOR

This book shall start like any other great romance, historical fiction, or action sequence, by stating the truth and putting it out there before any of my students read it and try to correct me. The reality is that I hate the use of describing myself throughout this book with the terminology of "I." It drives me batty, as any of my students can attest! Most of my days as a high school teacher and college professor are spent telling students they should never use "I" in formal writing because no one really cares about their opinion. It is always about content and proof of research... So, as this book started to come to fruition, it dawned on this writer that it cannot be avoided! That is, I must use the blasted word to explain the why of the book and the hilarity of where it all comes from. After all, I am the teacher of so many amazing students for almost twenty years, who have given me more laughs than I can write about and more random thinking points than I ever thought necessary to contemplate. To be clear and to explain what this book is really about, it's about the all-knowing teenagers in my life who state things in class discussions so matter-of-factly (sourced, of course, from social media—TikTok is their favorite) that even I once found myself lying in bed trying to go to sleep but instead was up wondering, "Why did the presidential candidate in the 1800s' political cartoon look more like a crazy chicken than someone that mattered to history?"

I must start from the beginning of the creation of this book about Consuelo's class by stating that it was never my intention to write a book about my class discussions. At this point, if you do not know me personally, you are probably wondering why you will see "many, many times" throughout the book. She is, in fact, my alter ego, given to me by the one and only Walt Disney World Company. My love for Disney is immense, and it comes from my childhood trips to the theme parks and then from my career with Disney for 25 years! In 2020, a little thing called COVID shut down the world, which caused my Disney World to do massive layoffs. Here is where it gets weird… I worked there for twenty-five years in many roles, so I was very sad to find out that they would be laying off all seasonal cast members due to the pandemic. If that was not bad enough, when I received my official papers, it was addressed to "Consuelo." Confused by this, I contacted them to verify which one of us was saying good-bye. They stated over the phone it was "whoever the letter is addressed to!" My response was simple: "Whew, okay, good, I was scared it was me. But you might want to let Consuelo know in case she shows up for a shift only to be told, 'No, we laid you off. Thanks for the memories!' But alas, after verifying ID numbers, it was me that was no longer working for the mouse. When I announced the news to my students, friends, and family, they grabbed it and ran! Always used as the joke when something was said, not to call out my own, or if someone was playing around with me… Consuelo's class was born.

Since 2020, when the students returned to school after being home, it sometimes felt like all teachers were in a constant state of watching their students slowly get back into recalling brain information we knew they had… but lots of hours on the couch binge-watching Netflix had left that content deeply buried somewhere, and all teachers spent hours daily trying to find it. Consuelo's class began to take on a life of its own as there were more and more funny, class-stopping moments shared with you in these pages.

This is a great opening to get the mind thinking about how this book will go, just in time to see the titles of the chapters! I will warn you, though, that the chapters are truly irrelevant in this book because, to be honest, once the book is read, I would challenge anyone to try to figure out how to combine the randomness?

Enjoy! -Consuelo

Table Of Contents

CHAPTER 1

Maybe they DON'T Know it All

When I decided to become a teacher, it was to "mold our youth, teach them about the world they live in, make a difference..." I was not aware it would also include teaching how to tie shoes some days, reminding them to blow their nose instead of sniffling snot back, reviewing manners, and how to not interrupt... but my biggest lesson to teach when I started teaching high school was how to get kids to stop answering like they know it all! Oh, the stories I could tell about people I overhear in my classroom or in the hall while students engage with each other! This all-knowing air about them as they explain to each other the lessons of life!

Perfect example, I'm standing in the hall greeting my students as they come in one day, and two kids are walking towards me in what appears to be a very serious conversation. As they get closer, I hear one say to the other, "NO, you don't know, and that is what will have them stealing your money from your bank account at midnight when deposits go in!!" This, of course, requires me to meander in their direction because I suddenly NEED to adjust something outside on the wall so I can eavesdrop to learn whatever it is that will be stealing my money at midnight!! As I get closer, the real talk continues, as the one student looks more apprehensive about the validity of this statement and says, "I do not think anyone steals your money, and I also do not think there is a requirement to have that in your bank account." To which the other student looks to me to help bring it home, "Downey! Isn't it true that you absolutely have to have a savings account, checkbook account thing, and a debit card account, now to protect your money!"

"Well, you started off strong…" I said. Thus, my "changing the world one student at a time" now has me teaching basic banking skills to the class, which included me explaining that a debit card was drawn from your banking account and not a separate account, which then required images and examples. This was way bigger for them to absorb than a simple, "you were close" and move on. It led to a whole class discussion and "teachable moments" as our administrators love to say. Just for the record, banking is not in my purview of the history curriculum. See, sometimes I am reminded that even though they correct me all day long with their versions of life and history, maybe they don't know it all…

1. November 18, 2020

In Consuelo Downey's class today: (Student walking past student posters on the wall)

Student: Why isn't mine's up here?

Me: Mines?

Student: Yes? Mines? Where is it?

Me: "Mines" is not a word in that context.

Student: You are so wrong—let me ask an intellectual— Siri! Is mine's a word?...HA! It's a noun!

Me: Yes, as in "look at the coal mines"—that's a noun!

Student: Oh....I will never doubt you again!

Me: As it should be.

Edit: When I told the next class about the above exchange, one said, "It's right in my dictionary! Where mines at and I'll show you!"

2. November 19, 2020

Consuelo Downey's class thoughts: talking about the Open Range and Farmers Grange Movement

Student 1: Speaking of cows, I love steak! I will eat it any way but burnt!

Me: No, I could never order medium rare steak.

Student 2: You know you can't get Medium Rare in Texas?

Me: ...(pondering) I'm sorry, what did you just say?

Student: Yeah—you can't eat rare there.

Me: I assure you they have it in Texas... there is no federal law that the whole world can have medium rare except Texas...

3. December 9, 2020

Today, back in Consuelo's class discussing World leaders, which led to favorite pizza.

Student 1: Oooh, Little Caesars is gross...

Me: Okay, where do you get your pizza from? (interrupted)

Student 2: Plus, their mascot is literally a caveman!!!

Me: What? Little Caesar's? (emphasizing the name slowly)

Student: Yes!

Me: Hello!!! It's Julius CAESAR FROM THE ROMAN EMPIRE!!!!

Student: What are YOU even talking about, Downey?

4. January 7, 2021

Background: talking about D-Day during WWII

Me: I was lucky enough to go to Omaha Beach in Normandy, France, where America landed. Here is sand from the actual landing area! (I know I'm a nerd.)

Student 1: It's just sand.

Student 2: How do you know that's sand from that beach?

Me: BECAUSE I was lucky enough to go there and collect it at the 75th D-Day celebration.

Student 2: Yeah, but how do you know that's the actual sand from the same beach?

Me: Ummmmm... sand stays on a beach...

5. January 22, 2021

Consuelo's Class: discussing history and media

Teacher prompt: The question is asking how you determine if the media is true or not while presenting information.

Me: Meaning how do you know what's real or fake news?

Student: Right! Like on Instagram (Gram) when it has a fact checker! Then you know it's legit!

Teacher: OH, MY GEEZ!!!

6. January 27, 2021

Consuelo's Class: discussing Harriet Tubman

Student 1: Downey, did you hear that they are reviving putting Harriet Tubman on the $20.00 bill?

Student 2: HEY! Isn't that the railroad lady? Right?

Me: I mean... you're not wrong, ish....

Student 3: Didn't she free the slaves?

Student 4: And... didn't she kill people if they didn't go with her?

Me: Sometimes you guys amaze me with your knowledge... then there are these moments when you have some pieces... but it's not quite in the right context.

Student 1: Check your sources, Downey.

7. January 28, 2021

Consuelo's class discussion: talking about students working jobs while going to school; they do not think it's fair any child has to do it. This came after I said,

Me: When I was a lifeguard in high school, we would have to shock the pool...

Student 1: Like with electricity?

Me: Yes! Yes, we would plug in a vacuum and throw it in the pool!

Student 2: Did they get out then?

(I am now deciding whether to roll my eyes, laugh out loud, or look for a new job)

8. March 31, 2021

This is today's opening question for class, which of course opened an interesting dialogue... but most random answers:

Student 1: I would want to go back in time to be one of Tupac's girls.

Student 2: I would go way back to the 90's century.

Student 3: I'm going back to the 20's when the Gitsies were popular!

Me: Gitsie?... you mean gypsy?!

Student 3: No, I do not! Gitsie!

Student 4: Do you mean Gatsby???

Student 3: Oh yeah! That!

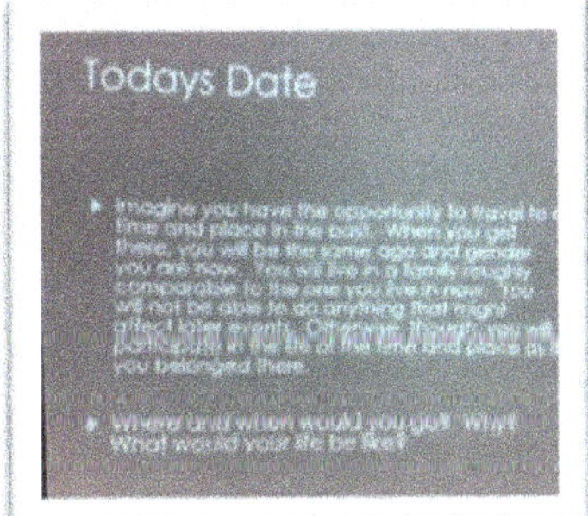

9. March 31, 2021

Consuelo's class again today... class has not even started when this conversation happens.

Student: Mrs. Downey, I'm about to get souvenirs for my teeth!

Me: You're doing what?

Student: Yeah, Ms! No cap! Souvenirs are gonna look good!

Me: Do you mean Veneers?

Student: (thinking…) Hmmmm, you may be right.

10. April 5, 2021

Consuelo's Class: (answering the daily question about how movies can teach us about historic events)

Student 1: Captain America!

Student 2: UMMM!!! He's not real, and if he was, he was in World War II!

Student 1: He is not?! But he was during the Cold War because he dies in the cold thingy…

Me: (just shake my head)…

11. May 19, 2021

Consuelo's Class moments… (Grading Cold War quizzes)

Question #2: How long did the Cold War last?

Student response: 45 years of very cold winters

Question #14: How did the Soviet launch of Sputnik impact the U.S?

Student response: "The US was very sad, and a lot of people cried, and so we got scared of Russia and shot Sputnik down to get even."

Me…. thinking maybe I should give partial credit for creativity?!?!

12. August 12, 2021

Summer is over and class is in session!

Today's question: What is the National Anthem of the United States of America?

Student 1: National Song

Student 2: National Anthem

Student 1: Don't be dumb! It's **THE** National Anthem

Student 3: Oh, Say Can You See!

Me: Guys, it's the Star-Spangled Banner

Student 1: No, I don't think that's it… that's a bad clue.

13. **November 3,2021**

Today, the in-class drama…. Question posed to kids:

If you could set one rule for your family that ALL must follow, what would it be and why did you choose this?

Student: They need to close the light when they leave the room!

All of us: What?!

Student: Close the light!

Me: Ummmmm, do you mean turn off the light???

Student: That's definitely what "close" means, Downey!

14. **November 15,2021**

Class discussion on the Roaring twenties: (The below picture is shown)

Me: What are these items? Tell me what you see.

Student: An Insta Pot.

Me: That's a washing machine.

Student: Are you sure? Did you use that kind?

Me: Yes, I am that old. (No, I am not.) What else do you see?

Student: A phone.

Me: Why is this a big deal in the 1920s?

Student: It's wireless, Miss! I didn't realize it started that far back.

15. April 25, 2022

Consuelo's Class - (1960s Social, Political, & Economic chart - they must find 6 items that go under specific categories and justify why)

Student: Can I put the U2 Spy Plane Incident under social?

Me: You have to justify why you see it as social.

Student 1: Didn't it make people like "whoa, they shot down a plane"… like we saw it, right?

Student 2: I'm sure they streamed it, right???

Me: Streamed in the 1960s????

16. August 11, 2022

Well, first episode… 2nd day! Consuelo's class is back…

Me: Tomorrow we will be taking a quiz to see what you know about the basics of American history/government.

Student 1: What? Miss?!?! How do I study for history and government? What kind of questions are we talking…

Me: Calm down, it's for fun. Basic US history questions, most of which I assume you know… like who was the first President of the U.S.?

Student 2: (very confident in an elevated voice) Oh, I got this! ABRAHAM LINCOLN!

17. September 23, 2022

Consuelo Downey's Class:

Me: It's really important to learn significant things as they are through time periods so they can be seen as a whole picture.

Student: Like music for time periods!?

Me: Yes! Like that!

Student: Like the 80's Beatles! They set that whole time period, Ms!

Me: Ummmmmmmmm… (shaking my head)

18. October 7, 2022

Happy Friday from Consuelo's class:

Me: What did the first Alexander Graham Bell phone look like?

Student: Like a brick

Me: Kind of, more like a box.

Student: (while acting it out for me to better understand) You know, the big black one shaped like a brick—you have to pull the antenna out before you can talk!

Me: That would be the first car/cell phone!

Student: Are you sure, Ms.?

Me: Alexander G. Bell would be so sad right now…

Student: Who's that?

19. October 13, 2022

Consuelo's class never lets you down! (Class discussion about how the colonists at one point gave smallpox blankets to the Indians…)

Student: Didn't they give the colonists disease too?

Me: Yes, they did. We also know there was transferring of STDs between all of them.

Student 2: Like Chlamydia?

Student 3: No, Downey—didn't we get Chlamydia because George Washington slept with a llama?

All Students: (all loud!) WHAT? Are you serious? A llama? Gross!

Me: As I always tell you, may I please see the source where you got this information?

Student 3: I got you! Wait one second (types on her computer)…SEE! Oh! Wait! My bad! It was Columbus with a sheep!

Me: Source?

Student 3: Right here! (walks towards me)

Me: Is it a reliable source, as in credible, as in scholarly? You know what I mean—can it back its statement up? (Shows me some generic fast and funny facts page) (reading…) This says a theory on a .com page! NOT RELIABLE!

Student: D%$*! I hate when you make us use smart sources!

20. Feb 9, 2023

Consuelo's class was in full effect today! (Discussing the Turn of the Century Amendments)

Me: What is the 18th Amendment?

Student 1: Prohibition.

Me: Why did the government feel this was important to pass the prohibition of alcohol?

Student 2: Because there were more cars being made, and they used gas—and alcohol is gas for cars! Right, Downey?

Me: I think you might be a little off…

Student 2: Nope! I'm confident!

21. September 20, 2023

Consuelo's class: 2 stories today…

Student: I was so gag!

Me: What does that mean? You are using it wrong!

Student: No, it's a thing!

Me: Why do you all keep trying to change the meaning of words? Use the correct vernacular!

Student 2: What does vernacular mean?

Student 3: It's another word for spectacular, dummy!

22. September 25, 2023

Consuelo's class (taking notes about the Transcontinental Railroad and the Golden Spike in Promontory Point, Utah…)

Me: The original Golden Spike is now in a museum near the connecting point…

Student 1: (randomly says) That makes me think of a golden bell… it has a crack in it, and I think it's important to America…

Me: Are you asking me what it is or telling me?

Student: I just know we learned about a golden bell once…

Me: The LIBERTY BELL?

Student: Yeah, maybe. Is it near the golden spike? Like they did a set?

23. January 10, 2024

In case you missed it… Consuelo's class moments:

Student 1: Wait, Downey, the Roaring 20's is the 20's?

Me: Yes… (shaking my head)

Student 2: Can you believe that 2024 to the Roaring 1920's… was a thousand years ago! That's CRAZY!

(And then we all waited to see how long it would take to see his error…)

We waited… and waited…

Student 3: (someone finally) "1000 years? Do you mean 100?"

Student 1: Ummm, look who's wrong now...

Student 2: You definitely mean 100.

Student 1: PROVE IT! Show me on a calculator!

24. **March 6, 2024**

Consuelo's class (discussing the Coal Miners' Strike 1919; groups are broken into groups to discuss their side vs. management (me)

Me: So, your group is asking for better safety measures. What about Canary? It has already been established that when the carbon monoxide level is low Canary tells you..."

Student 1: Wow! That job is awful. We need to ask that management guarantee more money for canary or the family in the bargaining.

Me: Why would they get more money?

Student: Because we send canary in... he dies... so we don't go in. That's a huge ask....

Me: YOU do realize "A CANARY" is a bird, right? ...

Student: Wait, what?!?!... I thought that was a guy.

CHAPTER 2

Holiday Vibes

When I first started in the classroom in 2005, I was an elementary school teacher, and they loved all things decorated, dressed up, hugs, high fives, you name it. So, the holidays were always a lot of fun with them. I am pretty sure everyone wishes they still got to make Valentine bags out of the white lunch sacks with the red heart doilies you glued on with too much glitter! Then you would drag your parents to the store to pick out the perfect box of Valentine cards to go around and drop the little cards in your classmates' bags; of course, giving your favorite to the person you liked!

But I digress. When I made the switch to teaching high school, I remember wondering if they would still love all things holidays and decorated rooms, and even teachers dressing up to match whatever day it was to celebrate. I found out quickly that they were still kids and still loved stickers for an assignment well done, candy as a treat, and the holidays! What I do not think they ever expected was me—over the top for all of it! I have dresses, socks, bows, tennis shoes, watch bands, costumes; you name it for every single holiday, and my students actually wait to see what it is that I will wear throughout each month! A little side note here: nothing makes me happier than the first time my students see "the Thanksgiving turkey dress." Their reaction is shocked, followed by maybe not so surprised! The fun part is when my students try to outdo me for different spirit days and holidays and try to get our administrators to judge all of us to see who wins. In the spring of 2024, the school did a spirit day where the teachers and students swapped, and my entire class asked to borrow all my holiday garb so they could be "Downey's" for the day, so I guess I am making some kind of impact! For me, it's just a simple life's pleasure to make us all smile by giving out good holiday vibes!

1. September 29, 2020

(While teaching the Civil War and mentioning that Savannah, Georgia, was a "Christmas gift" to President Lincoln from General Sherman.)

Student 1: So, Lincoln could talk to his people during the war?

Me: Yes, of course! In fact, he was very active in what was happening on the battlefield from where he was in D.C.

Student 2: Why did it take so long to get plans to people? Couldn't they just fax it?

(Class is giggling)

Me: As in fax machine?

2. November 20, 2020

Consuelo's class today:

Me: Today we will partake in a holiday tradition for Thanksgiving that is currently against the law in some states—not really...

Student: You mean Hanukah?

Me: ... Ummmmmmm... not exactly

3. May 5,2021

(Today is Cinco de Mayo, as most of the world knows, and yes, I am festively dressed in a fiesta shirt with tacos on it (of course), and this is the conversation that took place.)

Student 1: What's the date?

Student 2: The 5th of May.

Student 3: Mrs. Downey—it's Wednesday—aren't you supposed to dress up like that on Taco Tuesday?

Me: IT'S THE 5th! As in Cinco de Mayo...

Student: Ohhhhhhhh yeah, okay, that makes sense... nice taco socks, Downey!

4. December 2, 2021

Consuelo's Class: Teaching Great Depression and explaining the banking system and inflation by using the Twelve Days of Christmas to show how cost has changed over time

Me: Let's listen to a quick 3-minute episode on inflation and how it has affected the items of the Twelve Days of Christmas… (class is listening)

Student: (When the video is done, the student yells very animatedly) WAIT! What?! These are real things???

5. December 14, 2021

Consuelo Christmas class (Playing Christmas Trivia 🎄)

Me: What gifts did the Three Wise men bring baby Jesus?

Student 1: This should totally be a Spanish kid question.

Student 2: A camel!

Me: A camel? (Laughing)

Student 2: Yeah, I thought they rode it over there and gave it to him!

6. November 14th, 2022

Teaching the Roaring Twenties

Me: How do you think they may have celebrated the holidays like Thanksgiving during the Roaring Twenties?

Student 1: No one did!

Student 2: Yes they did, with the Indians!

Me: That was not exactly the right time period; you're thinking maybe the 1st Thanksgiving with the Pilgrim's and the Indians.

Student 2: So, what, they just stopped inviting Indians to Thanksgiving when they stopped wearing Pilgrim outfits or something?

Me: We are just going to skip this question for now…

7. April 2023

Reviewing for End-of-course exam

Teacher Prompt on board: Name a world event in American history that coincided with a major holiday and caused people to completely stop the event to celebrate.

Student 1: The Super Bowl!!

Me: No, while a good guess, think world event, lots of people involved, they stop what they are doing to come together in NO MAN'S LAND to exchange gifts and sing songs... (I am thinking this is a brilliant clue)

Student 2: If it's No Man's Land, then no one can be there. She is asking us a trick question!

Me: No, I'm not. One more clue: think Christmas.

Student 1: I got it! New Year's! Everyone celebrates that and sings the New Year's song!

Me: (feeling very defeated) No, World War I.

Student 3: Is that a clue too? Because no one sings during war.

Me: I give up...

CHAPTER 3

Questions & Advice from all Knowing Teens

The funniest part about working with high school kids is listening to them try to give each other advice because they simply have not lived long enough to have the experiences to actually compare anything to. So, every situation, is new, but in a teenage hormonal world, everything is much more dramatic! As all of us "old people" can attest to, we definitely know much more now than we did back in high school! I am sure when I was their age, my teachers listened to my friends and me talking and thought the exact same things, which now, some of those ideas seem completely hysterical. If I had known it all in high school and my parents had let me do whatever I wanted, I would be walking around today with a tattoo of Abu the monkey from Aladdin on my shoulder. Because in my infinite wisdom at the ripe age of 16, that was going to look amazing! But alas, I had those types of parents that cared and were always involved and said no and ruined my chance to be super popular by winning every argument by saying, "As long as you live under my roof…"

One of the 'big advice' that the students give each other that I hear often, is someone telling someone else what they have to do to get people to really know you love them! At least once a month, I will overhear one student tell another that "yes, it is a good idea to get your boyfriend/ girlfriends' name tattooed on you!!" Can you imagine if they actually followed this advice?? How many tattoos they will have by the time they are 20 years old?

Then, there is the other advice that I find odd that they all tell each other. If you are mad at anyone, whether it be a friend, family (parents included in this), or significant other, and they make you mad,

17

you should block their number on your phone and all social media, then ignore them until the next day or until they have tried harder than you to get back in touch. This I find completely insane for two reasons. The first is simply that if everyone is doing this to each other, then how do you know who is supposed to make the first move? I mean to say, you could be waiting a long time. Or is there an unwritten rule that at the 24-hour mark everyone just knows to unblock each other? And if you have followed this plan and the 24 hours is up, are you still supposed to be mad, or is everything fine again? The second reason to me seems pretty obvious: what if the person never reaches out to you again? Then who looks dumb!

This is why I could not follow their advice… so many questions from something that is supposed to help me be more calm but instead, I am having a panic attack because no one is contacting me, and I have no idea when the fight is over. But bigger than that is that based on their advice, I am ignoring and blocking someone that I just got the name of tattooed on my leg!! This all just seems so silly to me…

1. December 1,2020

Class Dating Advice during a Pandemic:

Student: I'm not going to lie Downey, if I pull down my mask, that means a girl better take down her mask, you know, so I can see what they really look like.

Downey: Shallow… prepare to be single for a while.

Student 2: I'm not gonna lie… some girls have beautiful 1/2 faces at this school…

(Whole class is laughing)

Student 1: Low key, Downey… you think someone's pretty… they take down their mask… AND BAM! You fell in love with someone missing 10 teeth.

2. January 28,2021

Before class, students are giving each other life advice, saying, "Bruh, you just gotta SALTS."

Student 1: SALTS!

Me: What the heck does SALTS mean for texting?!

Student 1: Smiles a little then stopped!

Me: How lazy!

Student 1: When I don't want to respond but it's smile-worthy!

Me: I would just answer "PEPPER"

Student 1: I don't think you get it Downey.

3. April 27,2021

Consuelo's class discussing the Cold War and different accents found during McCarthyism.

Student: Downey, how do you inherit an accent? I really want one!

(just speechless… standing there staring wide-eyed)

4. August 13,2021

Consuelo Downey's class discussing socialism.

Today's class prompt: Do we, as Americans, deserve free college or free medical care?

Student 1: Yes, and free condoms and tampons.

Me:(Now the challenge to control the class losing it…as everyone begins to debate what is more important: tampons, college, or condoms.)

5. October 22,2021

Speaking on "allies" during the Civil War and using the example of neighboring schools

Me: Whatever the school in Osceola is called… Ticonderoga something or other (students laugh)

Student: STOP! I thought Ticonderoga was only a pencil.

Me: (laughing out loud) I literally just taught you about Fort Ticonderoga in the Revolutionary War...

Student: Hmmmm I should probably listen better...

Me: Yes, that would be my suggestion (laughing)

6. December 2,2021

Consuelo's Class Teaching Great Depression and explaining the banking system and inflation etc. long story... but this is the short version:

Me: So, does everyone understand why I was upset? My deposited $10.00 cash was then given to my brother on a different transaction. Do you all understand what happens to your money when you deposit it into the bank?

Student: Yes, and you got upset for no reason Downey, because when you deposit money it gets added to your debit card, not the bank.

7. March 23, 2023

Consuelo Class resumed... (Background: Class is discussing the Cold War & Communism; one of the slides talked about the arms race between the U.S. & the Soviet Union.)

Me: Let's go back and review the "how" we got the atomic bomb and the "why" it bothered Joseph Stalin.

(Class discusses the decision for Truman to not utilize Stalin & Churchill's commitment to help from the Yalta Conference and how hard the decision would be to use a nuclear weapon....)

Student: Miss! I have really researched why Truman made the mistake with the bombs because Japan was going to surrender in a few days anyway.

Me: I know there is an argument to be had on both sides, and that's why I stress this was not an easy decision to make.

Student: But my research really looks into it and discusses why he shouldn't have. You should really check it out.

Me: Okay, I can do that. I have read both sides and am always open to more discussion.

Student: I think you will really like it. It's on YouTube....

Me: It's a documentary on YouTube—okay. What's the name of it?

Student: Shaun.

Me: S.H.A.W.N? Is that an acronym?

Student: No, Downey, it's a guy named Shaun. S... H... A... U... N... he is really smart!

CHAPTER 4

Making Fun of the Elderly

(And by this, I mean my age…48)

There is nothing more warm and fuzzy than standing in front of a classroom full of students, engaging in a great discussion happening all around, just to be stopped mid-sentence to be asked if "I remember when________ (insert an event that seems so inconceivable and choose that.) Now I have everyone's attention as they are either laughing at the statement or laughing, wondering if maybe I

am that old, thereby now having a whole room full of students looking at me while I have to make a split-second decision of whether I need to respond with sarcasm or call for guidance to come assist me for emotional support!

This is a biweekly "happening," and while I do reluctantly admit that I am no longer a spring chicken, I am definitely not filling out my application for retirement anytime soon. Students cannot comprehend that just because the person in front of them is teaching about history does not mean they actually lived through all of history, as if I was actually there when the Constitution was signed! Sometimes, I find myself having to sit down while having the student repeat their statement to try to clarify what was asked, because maybe, just maybe, I misunderstood them, or maybe they actually meant to say something else. But sadly, no… as I wait in hopeful anticipation that they will self-correct, they double down, stating, "No, that's what I meant.

Aren't you that old?" … now debating whether I will cry myself to sleep, I reluctantly bite my tongue while speaking through gritted teeth and state sweetly, "No, honey, I am not that old!" Oh, to be young again and assume 35 is an old person!

1. November 3, 2020

Student: I think people over 70 should not be allowed to vote.

Me: You do realize that cuts out a large portion of our government, right?

Student: No way!

Me: Someone look up the average age of Congress. (pause)

Student 2: 61.8 years old.

Student 1: No way! But younger people are more informed because we are on social media all the time.

Me: (biting my tongue and walking over to the 1940s on my timeline and just walking and pointing to all the history as I go since that time.)

2. November 16, 2020

Student 1: Did y'all know that Bill Nye the Science Guy is still alive?

Me: Yes.

Student 1: MISS! He has to be so old—like 60-something.

Student 2: Because really, 30 is old now, Miss!

3. August 30, 2021

Consuelo's Class today:

Student: Miss, if you dye your hair, it only lasts a few days, right?

Me: No, it lasts a while.

Student: I don't think so, Miss, because you're not all the way up in the ages, so you probably don't have to do it a lot, right?

Me: Somebody better send me a counselor; I'm being bullied.

(For reference - he says "up in the ages" is actually 70.)

4. November 2,2021

Conversation comes up before class about the iPhone.

Me: iPhones came out in 2007

Student: That wasn't the first phone, Miss.

Me: I am aware… my first phone was a bag phone, and before that it was a dollar store phone filled with candy. I used it at red lights to look cool to other drivers!

Student: You're wrong about the Apple date!

Me: How do you know?

Student: Because it came out in 2006… when I was born.

Me: Kill me now! (As I take out the original iPhone to show them, to which someone asked if it was a real "relic.")

5. November 2023

Consuelo Downey's class talking about the Model T invention.

Student 1: Mrs. Downey, was it weird when the car came around?

Me: Are you asking me what the people felt like or if I remember how it felt for cars to come around?

Student 1: No, like one day you're walking and taking a buggy, and the next day you're cruising with friends?

Me: Are you asking me if I took a horse to school until cars came out?

Student 1: (says emphatically) YES!

Me: (getting louder as my questioning goes) When did the Model T come out? What years are we talking about?? HOW OLD DO YOU THINK I AM???

Student: Calm down, Downey, sheesh!

(Again, pondering a new career… this is killing my self-esteem!)

6. April 10, 2024

Consuelo's Class: (Talking about the 1960s and Woodstock)

Me: So, Woodstock—3 days of music and rock & roll, amongst other things…

Student: Yeah! Like Limp Bizkit! I bet they were amazing!

Me: They were not at Woodstock in the 1960s.

Student: I'm pretty sure you're wrong… I know I heard something about them being there. Weren't you there? Don't you remember?

7. September 13, 2024

Consuelo's class - a group of students asking me a question before class in the hallway.

Student 1: Do you remember way back when you were in high school?

Me: It's not really way back, but yes.

Student 2: Okay, so we have a question. (Me nodding my head for her to continue.) Did you all have football games back then?

Me: For Pete's sake! How old do you think I am? Of course we had football games! Those were around way before me!

Student 1: It's okay, Downey, you don't have to be embarrassed!

(BULLYING AGAIN!!?? I can't handle much more.)

8. August 2024

While clearing the hallway and bathroom right before the one-minute bell

Me: Come on ladies, let's get going; you have less than a minute. (I notice there are three sets of feet in one stall, which normally is not a good sign.)

Me: All right - let's get out! Why are there three people in the stall?

Student 1: (inaudible grumbling)

Student 2: Sometimes it just happens!

Me: What just happens?! Are you all just happening to accidentally end up in the same stall?

Student 3: Downey, don't you ever go to the restroom with your girlfriends?

Me: Restroom? As in the whole place? As in standing outside waiting near the mirrors? Yes, but never in the same stall! That's weird.

Student 2: You don't get it because you're older than us.

(Seriously?!?! How did three in a stall make me old again???)

CHAPTER 5

Sometimes You Just Need to Laugh

Sometimes the funniest moments happen in class at the most inopportune times, and no matter how hard I try to stop the momentum, the worse it seems to get for the students to try to contain themselves. In a typical school year, vested teachers have one formal observation along with four or five informal observations, where an administrator will just pop in during class time. They will watch for a minute or two, see what the students are working on, and how you interact with the class. It's very simple, and they typically do not speak but will mark you off as visited on a rubric to show you how you are doing; it is in no way a got you 'walk-through'. But just to be safe, from day one, all teachers have taught their kids to be on point when any administrators walk through the door, all of us telling them that they cannot make us look bad!

On this particular day, my students were working at their tables, doing a class discussion with source checks. I was at the front of the room near the door and was not paying attention to the window for any activity in the hallway. As the roaring twenties discussion continued, a student asked me about how flappers were 'freer' with themselves than before.

Me: Truth is there are modern changes that allowed it. Flappers were a new type of woman; they held jobs, wore more makeup, challenged social norms they liked dating instead of courting, and they mingled in speakeasies drinking with men, which was new.

Student 1: So, they were "bad" girls?

Students 2: (before I can answer) So, easy?

Me: No! Just flirty and fun and more open to ideas that maybe would not have been there before.

Student 1: It's okay Downey, we get it.

Me: (Needing to get my point across, I raise my voice far louder than needed...) Guys! It is not like girls are standing outside Speakeasy's saying (door opens and in walks my principal, but I do not hear him...) "I like Alcohol & Sex!"

The class is staring at me wide-eyed as I turn to see my boss standing there with a blank stare on his face... Then, no longer being able to hold it, a symphony begins— the sound of students beginning to laugh, not all at once, but one by one, and not quietly, but instead very loudly, and with no restraint! As they are losing their minds and I am standing there deciding whether to laugh or cry, the principal shakes his head with no expression, so I say, "Would you like my resignation now?" He keeps staring at me and turns to walk outside, and as the door closes behind him, my principal busts out laughing down the hall! Just a typical day in the classroom, and if I don't just laugh with it, I would probably go crazy!

1. December 2, 2020

Meanwhile, back in class... sometimes trying to keep from laughing hysterically is soooo hard! ...Let me set today's scene—students are analyzing historical documents for meaning. We are looking at a political cartoon from World War I; the Zimmerman note, and the students were discussing how we know the person portrayed was Mexican...

Me: Notice specific things added to indicate the person's background.

Student 1: Like the guy's hat shows he's German.

Me: Correct.

Student 2: The other guy is Mexican because he has on a sombrero and poncho.

Me: Yes, good—the sombrero…

Student 3: (interrupting me loudly) DOWNEY! I like the ones with the little ding-a-lings that hang down!

(All guys in class start to giggle, and I am smiling under my mask.)

Me: You mean…

Student 3: (interrupting again…) I mean the ones with fuzzy balls hanging down! Those are my favorite because I like playing with them…

Me: (now laughing out loud, and the… whole class erupts into laughter, and now I am no longer in

control…)

2. October 29, 2021

OH GEEZ! Consuelo's strikes again!

Student: Downey! Where were you yesterday?

Me: At a training at Bartow High School.

Student: What was the training about?

Me: How to be a good social studies teacher.

Student: Haven't we already taken social studies?

Me: This is a social studies class.

Student: I swear I took it already but anyway, did you get punished or something and have to go to this training?

Me: No, I did not get punished!

Student: Are you sure??? You can tell us!

3. November 5, 2021

Consuelo's class is working on Content Summaries. Note: I make my students write all vocabulary words in cursive. Why? Because it's a lost art no longer taught, and let's be honest, they need to know how to at least sign a signature.

Student: Can you write nineteen in cursive, Miss?

Me: Yes, I can also write 20 and 76 as well...

Student: (to another student) So there IS cursive numbers! I told you stupid!

Me: (crying because I need to retire, and because I now have to explain numbers are numbers)

4. January 6, 2022

All classes are doing a WW2 map activity.

Situation 1:

Students must color all water on the map blue.

Student: There is water in the land? Is that land-water?

Me: Noooooo, it's a lake!

Teacher 2: Can you go to Publix and ask where the land water is kept, Mrs. Downey?

Me: (laughing) Yes, they will say it is near the spring water?!

Student: I don't get your humor teachers!

5. February 25,2022

So long since Consuelo's class stopped me in my tracks... (Discussing war and if men could be drafted if they were the only sons and carrying on the name, etc...)

Teacher: If my son doesn't have a son, the name Downey dies.

Student 1: "What if Alexandra keeps her name? Then it would keep going."

Teacher: "Not biologically, she could use it as a middle name but then it would sound weird like two last names."

Student 1: "No, it wouldn't. ROBERT DOWNEY JUNIOR."

(SILENCE… then laughter…)

Student 2: "Ummmm, did you think Junior was his last name??"

Student 1: "NO!… yes… Isn't it?"

6. March 17, 2022

If people don't think phones and social media distract children as much as we say—chew on this data from today…

Student: Downey—may I put my phone on your desk during the test?

Me: Yes! (Phone light and vibrations start going off immediately and non-stop) "This is why you cannot concentrate… your phone never stops notifying you…"

Student: It's not that bad Downey!

(So I start to count while students test…)

Results:

Me: From 1:10 to 1:55, you got 213 notifications sent to you!!!!

Student: I know, it's a slow day!

7. April 6, 2022

Playing trivia with students:

Me: William Penn founded a colony now known as which state?

(Waiting… waiting)

Students: We don't know…

Teacher: Listen to the name… William PENN!

Student: Pennsylvania?

Me: (sarcastic) Yes! Great job!

Student: Why would any parent name their child after a state? That's dumb…

8. April 25, 2022

Consuelo's Class:

(Topic - Betty Friedan, The Feminine Mystique, Gloria Steinem, and Ban the Bra)

Student: I wouldn't burn my bra but I also wouldn't wear it to bed! Wearing your bra to sleep is like wearing socks to sleep!

Me: Sometimes moving on QUICKLY is the best way to end strange comments in class…

9. August 12, 2022

Consuelo's Class - Test your knowledge of the founding…

Me: What is our National Anthem?

Multiple Students: O say, can you see!

Whole class: By the dawn's early light… what so proudly we…

Me: Yes, that is it and while I love a good sing along and that you all know the words… I am looking for the actual name.

Student: We just told you- it's O Say, Can You See!

10. September 8, 2022

Consuelo discussion before class

Student: If you lie about your transcripts, isn't that FRAUDERY?!?!

Me: I'm sorry, what?

Student: Isn't it FRAUDERY?

Me: I'm sorry, what? (What do you say to that?)

Student: Like, committing fraud - it's the action of.

Me: It's just fraud; it does not become its own hero verb.

Student: Fraudery sounds cooler!

(I can't disagree.)

11. October 13, 2022

Talking about socialism related to other countries…

Student: Socialism sucks? Wait… what is socialism? Like talking too much???

Me: (laughing) So close, but no!

12. November 7, 2022

Consuelo's class 7:26a.m.: (Students are studying primary documents about WWI)

Student: MISS! (Always yells it) How long has US history been alive?

(Class bursts out laughing)

Me: (stares into the abyss, mouth agape… contemplating my career choice!)

13. January 14, 2023

Consuelo's assignments can be tough… (The Assignment - students will choose any topic about World War II (not a person) to research and write a formal paper about.)

Student: Miss… I don't get it….

Me: Don't get what?

Student: The assignment… any topic of WW2?

Me: Okay - how can I help?

Student: I had an idea, but my sister said I'm dumb…

Me: Okay, what is it?

Student: A paper about the dead bodies after the war. You know, what they do with them.

Me: They bury them.

Student: Oh. I probably can't make 1-6 pages out of that…

** Let me add this edit because a valid thought has been said. After my sarcastic answer, I did inquire if he, in fact, was looking to learn about the actual process and decisions made. He simply said, "Nope! Just hoping for a short paper." **

14. May 8, 2023

Consuela's Class today (Background: Working on the End of Course Review and a group is talking about Imperialism)

Student 1: Isn't this time period have something to do with colonizing... yes, I think that's it.

Student 2: It's a little more (before they can finish)

Student 1 to 2: Are you white? I don't feel like you are...

Student 2: What do you think?

Student 3: I could see someone saying from the islands.

Me: I could see that - like Polynesian!

Student 1: What? You mean like the sauce? That's dumb Downey!

Me: (others laughing LOUDLY) ... UMMMM... no, Polynesian like the islands, you know Hawaii....

Student 2: Like Maui.

Student 1: He's Hawaiian - not the color of sauce idiot!

15. May 9, 2023

TWO DAYS IN A ROW! Still reviewing for tomorrow's big test...

Me: (talking about supply & demand) So this is when we see farm prices increase.

Student 1: Like now with farm prices increasing, Downey?

Me: Yes, exactly the same. If we have a surplus in farm production, the cost of items will go down.

Student 2: I hate inflammation! It's impossible to stop it!

Me: Sure there is! Ice it and take some Tylenol—that should help a lot. (Class laughing)

Student 2: Oh, like that's really gonna work!

16.September 19, 2023

Consuelo's class: Today was a holding day, and while babysitting a few classes together, the students collaborated on an Amendment activity. During a presentation a student walks to the front of the class; he has on black jeans and a black t-shirt with an older picture of Dolly Parton with the top simply reading "Dolly."

Me: So, do you like Dolly Parton?

Student: Who?

Me: Dolly on your shirt?

Student: oh. No.

Teacher (laughing): Do you know who it is on your shirt?

Student: Nah, it just goes with the fit.

Me: (Laughing and shaking head) What the heck?!!…Just wrong!

Student: Nah, the fit looks great!

17.September 20, 2023

Students notice a bobblehead of Polk County Sheriff Grady Judd on the bookshelf.

Student: Who is that?

Me: Sheriff Grady Judd.

Student 1: Is there only one sheriff for Polk County?

Me: Yes. It's him.

Student 2: I think you're wrong Downey, there's more here I think because I've seen lots of cars that say "Polk County Sheriff" on it.

18.September 21, 2023

Consuelo's Class: Reminding students of the directions.

Me: Remember, we have to pick EXACTLY 10 items to load onto "your" Conestoga Wagon to move west. Only take what is essential! No, you cannot say "phone and charger!"

Student 1: A pound of granola.

Student 2: Dried fruit.

Me: Good, Remember, only 10.

Student 3: Wait! Are there stoves in the wagons? I need to be able to cook!

19. November 3, 2023

Consuelo's Class:

Me: Teddy Roosevelt was a major hunter and, in fact, liked taxidermy. Quick reminder, what is taxidermy?

Student 1: When they stuff animals.

Student 2: Can't we do that with people? Someone must have that job, right?

Me: (just stunned) Never a dull moment

20. November 2023

Student: "Yes! I know who Teddy Roosevelt is! He made Bears!"

Me: "Bears? As in the animal?"

Student: "Yes Downey! The Bear as in GRRRRR!" (while holding up his hands as paws)

Me: "No, I assure you the bear, was here long before Teddy Roosevelt."

Student: (looking to his tablemates)

"I think she is wrong!"

21. March 22, 2024

Consuelo's Class doing centers for contracts today. A student is struggling with a word…

Teacher: What does relic mean?

Student: I am thinking of a condiment!

Teacher: (trying so hard not to laugh as they realize they are thinking of relish) No, that's not it.

22. April 2, 2024

Consuelo's Class (talking about giving back and doing things that are bigger than yourself. Without technology!)

Teacher: I need you to think of ways to give of yourself. Your generation does everything for social media.

Student: I do good things; I once bought my boyfriend dinner.

Teacher: Okay… I need you to think about others YOU Don't know and think of ways to give of your time. I invite you to go to any Veterans hospital this summer and help in any way they need.

Student: You mean like animals…

23. April 11, 24

Consuelo's Class Moment (Learning about Civil Rights - working on creating presentations for the Civil Rights Movement. Picture below)

Student 1: Downey I am doing group 3, and I am not sure how to look up Ark Sit-Ins.

Teacher: Excuse me? I didn't understand - what are you asking?

Student: I'm in charge of "Ark," and all I can find is a video game…

Teacher: (after some time of really being confused about what he was asking, I look to the PowerPoint and try not to fall out of my chair from rolling my eyes, knocking me off balance…) Please read all of number 3 to me.

Student: Table 3: Little Rock, Ark & Sit-Ins

Teacher: (realizing I will just have to explain because they are not getting it) Little Rock, Ark**ANSAS** as in the place.

Student: How does anybody know that, Miss?

Teacher: Okay… wait… so if the group divided it up… what were you all thinking about putting for Little Rock in regard to Civil Rights?

Student 2: It was hard Mrs. Downey. We were trying to find the rock involved in any event, and we can't!

24. August 26th, 2024

Here we go!!!! Consuelo's class dismissal addition! (Students are all leaving for the day, and I am answering questions.) All of a sudden, I hear:

Student 1: I said, "Will I get an A?" (So, I look to see who or what is being talked about.)

"Okay fine! I will ask this…" leans into an item and speaks louder.

"IS THIS EVEN ON? How do I get it to work?!"

Me: (It is then that I realize the student is yelling at an old-school 8 BALL! )

This was such a pleasure to write and share with my students, their parents, and many others—just to take a minute to make everyone smile! The students are the best at laughing at themselves when these moments happen, laughing even more when they see me write it down, and then always jumping in to talk since these moments are always followed with great class discussions. I can tell you, as long as I work with students, these great moments will continue to happen! The truth is, There Will Never Be a Dull Moment with Consuelo's (Downey's) History Class!